Glimpses

Cathleen Meisberger

Presentation by *BookLeaf Publishing*

Web: www.bookleafpub.com

E-mail: info@bookleafpub.com

ISBN: 9789357748841

First edition 2023

I dedicate this book to my husband and my daughter. You are the reason I do everything. You are the reason I try my best. You are the reason I never quit. I love you both more than words could ever do justice.

ACKNOWLEDGEMENT

I would like to thank my husband Brian, for always indulging all of my wild ideas. I would love to thank my friends for always being my sounding board, my cheerleaders, and for giving me honest critiques. And lastly, I would love to thank my daughter Arya for inspiring me to try whatever it is, I want to try.

Nothing like I thought you'd be

When I was just a little girl
I wondered what my life would be
What kind of job, type of car
and who would marry me
I pulled out a sheet of clean white paper
and grabbed my box of crayons
Then chose myself a color
and started drawing my perfect man
He had white skin and huge green eyes
his hair was blonde and wavy too
He was 8 feet tall, buff, with a sharp jaw
And this man looked nothing like you

Then I got a little older
Tried my drawing once again
I kept the green eyes, pale skin and blonde hair
But this time I made him thin
I made him look real hard and mean
A bad boy covered in tattoos
He had piercings, wore baggy pants, but man
could he dance
And he still looked nothing like you

A few years passed once again

and I had been away at school
I found my drawing and laughed myself to tears
I can't believe I thought that guy was cool
The man that I was seeing now
Was studying dentistry
He was a clean cut quiet catholic boy
And he wasn't really into me
He was someone to take to dinner parties
But was so boring, he could make me drool
He ironed his jeans, and starched his shirts
Yet again he looked nothing like you

Then I met you, and you were different
Than I ever imagined you'd be
You weren't the right height
and had a bit of a belly
And your skin was tattoo free
You had a slightly crooked smile
and a dimple on your chin
But you had the best laugh I'd ever heard
coming out of a boyish and wicked grin
You had kind blue eyes, and thinning brown hair
And you were madly in love with me
You look nothing like you were supposed to
But you looked like everything I'd ever need

A Child of You

I was sinking,
Drowning in sorrow.
Guilt had swallowed today
Shame threatened tomorrow
I couldn't see anything
I could hear nothing at all
I just sank further still
And continued to fall
Then an outstretched hand
appeared from above
it was clean and bright
Warm with grace and love
I grabbed it and held on
As tight as I could
You pulled me out of the water
And there we both stood
You'd beheld me with a smile
"Well done", You said
Then you wrapped your arms around me
As I rested my head
My heart expanded so wide
It barely fit in my chest
Your hold on me grew tighter
As you told me to rest
Though I had never met you before

I knew who you were
I could feel a shift happening
And I sensed my soul stir
Like a shattered glass puzzle
My broken pieces came together
I knew then, that my life
Had just changed forever
I came out of that water
A creation, anew
I was reborn that day
As a child of You

A Desperate Wish

All of my life my mother
Took care of young kids
Of all of her talents
Being a mom was her gift
She trained me and raised me
To follow her lead
She carefully picked
And planted the seed.
Maybe she subconsciously knew
She wouldn't be there by my side
To show me how it's done
When it was my time.

When I was a girl
Not so old at all
My mother gave me
My first cabbage patch doll
To most people this gift
Sounds no more than a toy
But his name was Andrew
And he was my little boy
I clothed him and groomed him
We were never apart
I was his mommy, his best friend
And he had my heart

As a teen I forgot
About my lifelong plan
I was more interested in friends
Than I was in a man
The day I'd be a mother
Was just too far away
I wasn't quite there yet
And that was ok

As I got older,
motherhood came back to mind
I could wait to start
But felt left behind
I watched friend after friend
As they said, "I do"
But I hadn't met my guy yet
There was no more I could do
Year after year passed
Nothing changed at all
I felt like Cinderella
But with no invitation to the ball

Then after I almost gave up
I met the man of my dreams
We fell in love and got married
So happy, I was bursting at the seams
I knew what would come next
We did everything right

I would think about meeting you all day
And dream of holding you all night

One after one
My friends had their kids
But not me, not yet
My baby remained only a wish
We tried and we tried
And months passed as they do
And each test had one line
When there should have been two
I asked my Doctor to help us
We did everything she said
But this doubt started creeping
Into my heart and my head
I knew something was wrong
My body, it seems
Cared nothing of my hopes
It ignored my begging and screams
Now I'm told there's no chance
What do I do with that?
I can't decide if I'm angry
Confused or just sad
What if I told you,
"Fuck whatever you thought
Give up all your life's plans
What you knew would be, will not"
I'll never get to meet you
There's not even a chance

Holding you in my arms
Has just slipped through my hands

If I could have been
Half the mother, my mom was
You would have spent your life showered
With kisses and love
Please just know that I love you
My sweet boy or beautiful girl
You are my purist wish
You would have been my whole world.
I believe someday I'll find you
Among the stars in the sky
I'll recognize you immediately
My heart will know you are mine
Until then I'll try to smile
Through the grief and the pain
And wait for the rainbow
That comes after the rain.

Back to Life

Goodbye old friend
I loved you once
Your smile so bright it hurt
Now you're dead and gone, you stayed too long
And now you lie deep into the earth
You were loud, and loved to laugh
and befriended everyone you ever met
your pain ran so deep, you'd even cry in your
sleep
you were someone I won't soon forget
You had to go, you had no choice
you'd overstayed your time
you had your fun, chased the moon and sun
Crossed every boundary, skipped every line.
The debt you owed had to be paid
It was time to become something new
You waved goodbye with a kiss, knowing we
will all miss
The extraordinary wonder of you
What you didn't know, is that you'd be back
but completely different than before
This time you are strong, and nothing feels
wrong
You are you but not you
so much more.

There is light that glows from inside
and you spread it everywhere go
your burden and shame burnt to ash, and left in
the past
While the new fire in you consistently grows.
The beauty found in ruin is only appreciated
by those who have survived the pain
Just like a storm will bring smiles, to those who
are wild
enough to sing and dance in the rain
So hello new friend, I'm so glad you are here
I wasn't sure I would ever see this day
But a caterpillar must die, for a butterfly to
arrive
And so now, you too can fly away

Jennifer

My sister was strong
and could sing like a bird
but her temper was quick
she could cut you with words
She was different than others
smarter than most
she had the blondest of hair
skin white as a ghost.
Her eyes were grayish-blue
She got those from our mother
We used to fight all the time
we could barely stand one another
she didn't know how
to navigate this cold world
she was unique and complex
not your typical girl
I was easygoing and charming
I fell into line
She longed for the life
that I'd claimed for mine
Her jealousy festered
then her fists flew left and right
Til my mother had no choice
But to get her out of our life
My sister turned to drugs

and other lost souls too
She burned bridges
with everyone else that she knew
But the ravers excepted her
loved her the best they knew how
She found herself a family amongst them
She felt lost to us now
Sixteen years passed
only reuniting for holidays
we'd make small talk then argue
retreating to our separate ways
Then one day she fell sick
worse than ever before
she spasmed and dropped
like a dead weight to the floor
It was cancer, they said
It had spread all around
My parents told me through tears
But I heard not a sound.
The world stopped turning
my sister was going to die
I couldn't breathe, couldn't think
I could not even cry
She was so young,
only thirty years old
this can't possibly be true
just a lie we've been told
They gave her four months
Eight months at best

Then her body would give out
and be laid to rest.
I was so angry
we'd lost so many years
we said so many sorrys
through buckets of tears
I cared for her
as much as I could til the end
then said goodbye to my sister
I wish we could have been friends
We will never get the time
to gain back what we lost
our pride came before our fall
at an unaffordable cost
I still think about Jennifer
how much she'll never get to see
How she'll never meet my family
or really ever know me
How she wasn't here when our Mom
left the earth the same way
How she won't be here to stand beside me
On our Father's last day
I hope we do get the chance
To be together again
To repair what was broken
My sister, my friend.

Arya

I love your sandy straight blonde hair
I cherish your button nose
I adore your expressive hazel eyes
I can't stay away from your ticklish toes
Your dimpled chin is so perfectly you
your smile could rival the sun
I admire your courage to try new things
you are so loved by everyone.
You are funny, smart and unafraid
You love so deeply with your whole heart
You're good at everything you try to do
I miss you every time we're apart
You are the best friend I always wanted
You also make me crazier than anyone else
I pray you never let the world change who you
are
and always stay true to yourself

Rapture

When it is time
for Your return
Don't worry about me,
Just please take her
I don't deserve
Your grace or your mercy
But if I could ask this one favor
even though I'm not worthy
Please don't leave her here
to suffer and be afraid
She knows not what she does
she is only a babe.
Collect her and keep her
safe up above
where she will feel no pain
and be filled with Your love
I'll pray on my knees
to see her once more
I'll praise and I'll worship
more than ever before
I'll wait patiently for You
as I wonder alone
to call Your humble servant
back to her home

Mothers and Daughters

There're times I've had to say hard things
Sometimes I have made you cry
When I've had to tell you no or not today
With no explanation why
Some days I can't hug or kiss you enough
though lately I've needed some space from you
That's hard for me to admit out loud
But that doesn't make it any less true
We drive each other mad at least once a day
as most mothers and daughters do
but you could search the world and still come up
short
trying to find one who loves you as much as I do
This is just a phase they say
of that, I'm not so sure
I remember the other side of this very coin
I've walked in similar shoes before
Yet my Mother and I survived this challenge
somehow
and came out stronger on the other side
With greater love and understanding
And a few deep scars that healed with time
There's hope for us yet, my little one
I love you more than you could ever imagine
I'd do anything to keep you safe from harm

I'd walk through the fires of hell and back again
The depth of my love won't stop us from
fighting
or keep me from telling difficult truths
Keeping you happy isn't my job, though it's nice
God chose me to raise the best version of you
Sometimes that will require we argue
Some days you will feel like you hate me
And even when I don't recognize who you've
become
You'll always be your Mama's baby.
So take my hand, daughter of mine
we'll take each day on, together, step by step.
We will do our best to lead with grace and love
And we'll let God handle the rest.

Healing

They refused to see
how badly you were hurt
what they put you through
leaving your heart scarred and burnt
They disrespected, and discarded you
like you meant nothing at all
They pushed and they laughed
as they watched you repeatedly fall
They expected you'd always
find your way back to your feet
To come back for more abuse
or to provide for their needs
Spoiled and reckless
hateful and cruel
They mocked and humiliated
and played you for the fool
But God had a plan
to show you what love could be
And He devised a time and place
that would lead you to me
With faith and perseverance
we broke your chains together
and made a vow to love
and protect each other forever
It didn't happen overnight

Wounds that deep heal with time
But the bleeding began to clot
when I called your heart mine.
They continued to try
to tear us wide open again
every olive branch we extended
was just torn into shreds
Then finally we decided
that we'd suffered enough
We chose to forgive them and let go
And walk away together in love
Family means more
than the blood that runs under your skin
It's who supports, defends and shows up for you
Again and again
I pray you always have the strength
to choose your own peace
You will never walk alone again
You have God, and you have me.

Toxic love

There I was standing next to you
where you left barely any standing room
Larger than life, more than I could ever be
And you were standing next to me
You acted as though you were doing me a favor
letting me taste the flavor
of your bitter but sweet lips
Oh what pain I endured
what did I do to deserve
such madness as this.
Even when I do all I can to get away,
you convince me to stay
You breathe me into your lies
That quick tongue and strong hands
Why can't I say no to this man
With his beautiful but deceiving eyes
I want to rip my heart out
which I cannot do
how much more must I endure
suffering through
Then you leave me exposed
completely alone
as you return back to her
Back to your false sense of salvation
your loveless consummation

leaving me here to burn
Now that you got what you wanted
you are holding me hostage
You forget I hold the match to burn you alive
You used my love for you against me
to hurt me immensely
weeping gasoline tears as I cry
You are breeding rage from desire
creating a fire
from which neither of us will escape
You come down on me,
but you won't set me free
you seem to take pleasure in watching my pain
But what you didn't see
is you mistook me for weak
you never thought I would ever bite back
How blind you must be
you never really knew me
if you thought I didn't plan my own attack
Without any warning
You'll wake up one morning
to find your world has burnt down around your
feet
And you'll see me with my match
head cocked back in a laugh
I'll say, "Now you know how it feels to be me."

On the contrary

I can't breathe.
I'm choking in on the tears that are just caught in
my throat,
along with everything I am dying to say I can't
put into sentences.
I've never been confronted with such sheer
ugliness in misery, and it's of my own fault.
I should have let things go once I saw your eyes
change, but I kept forcing the inevitable, and
then when it approached, damn me, I wasn't
ready for it.
So here I sit, shaking my head, wondering how
the hell this all happened.
How did they let you in? How did I let you
break me?
And you know you did too.
I was never good at explaining myself, even to
myself. I overanalyze everything, and I get
confused with every thought that runs through
the cobwebs that replaced my brain. What seems
like years ago.
I don't know what I want from you, or where this
is going. If it lasts the next five minutes, it will
have said something, and if it doesn't last the
next five seconds, it will have said it all already.

thank you for pointing out this weakness and
me, as if I wasn't overly conscious about it as it
is
A wave of exhaustion is coming over me, and I
realize that I can't be friends with everyone. Not
everyone is going to like me, much to make
continued confusion.
I'd have to implant myself into your eyes to see
how you see me, and then maybe I'd understand,
but till then, I can only shrug my shoulders and
continue to feel like I failed somehow. I'm not
gorgeous. I rely on who I am to attract people to
me, and I've been successful till I met you. You
don't let me get away and chime in with the loan.
You wanna dig deeper into my emotions and
soul. You want me to whisper my demons to
you, but you're one of them. Someone who
intimidates me and fascinates me all at once. I've
never lost control of myself until now, and I hate
it. And I appreciate it. So thank you, and fuck
you, all at once.
I never saw you coming, and I never saw you
wanting to go. But you have to blink sometimes,
I guess that's when the inevitable happened.

Mom

I have missed you
every day since you died
a holiday hasn't passed
that I haven't cried
Having my daughter
and watching her grow
without a grandma
she'll never know
You would have loved her
You would have taught her all you knew
about quilting and baking
and country music too
She would have seen my dad happy
instead of just a shell of who he was
I wish that you could visit
Instead of just observing from above
I wish that she could hear
your terrible singing voice one time
That she could laugh at something funny you
said
That she could know you outside of this rhyme
I wish that you could dance with her
since you both move slightly off beat
I wish you could offer her a bargain
that would result in her massaging your feet

I wish that she could hear your laugh
after a cocktail or two
I wish she could see you curled in your chair
with a book
I hate that she'll never meet you
She thinks that I'm the best Mom there is
But she never knew the Mom I did
How lucky she would have been to have us both
Had you been given the chance to live

Dad

I can't imagine
the pain you went through
saying goodbye to your daughter, your brother,
and then your wife too
Being forced to stay strong
while those you loved the most died
Watching as cancer stole them away
while you were left behind
As if that wasn't enough
you had to let your business go
your life's work became too heavy
a burden to hold
Then your body bit by bit
starting giving way to age
And your finances grew sparse
living on a very limited wage
You were lonely and broken-hearted
you had no one to come home to
I had moved away to start my own life
There wasn't anyone there to love you
But then God answered both our prayers
And a child was given to us
She made me a Mother and you a Pop pop
She reminded you what it felt like to love
She made you happy and smile once more

she cuddled as she curled up on your lap
She used her silly and loving nature
To bring my Father back.
I still see you crying in your living room
when something sad comes on
But you're still here, where I need you to be
When everything else seems wrong
I'm glad you have each other
I'm happy she brought back your glow
I'm thankful for this borrowed time we have
More grateful than you'll ever know.
I love you Dad, my hero
My first love, my first best friend
I know I can't replace all the people you lost
But I'll be with you til the very end.

Jesus

Your miracles in my life
made me lose my breath
You filled my soul
til there was nothing else left.
You pulled me out
from a life of sin
You changed my heart
I've been born again
You had a vision
for what I could be
so You broke my shackles
and set me free
I can't stop singing
praises to You
No one on earth
can do what You do
You are the perfect Father
You love so completely
Your Grace so undeserved
Yet given so freely
For this sinner You saved
I can't thank You enough
For rescuing me
For always leading with love
So now all I can do

Is whatever You ask
I'll live my life for You from my knees
I'll complete every task
I owe You more
than I'll ever be able to afford
You can have my life, my heart, my soul
It's all Yours
Thank You Jesus
For giving Your life on the cross
Even though You gave it all
It was not a loss
You saved everyone
willing to believe
Not just the good, and the helpless
You even saved sinners, like me
Thank You Jesus
For the blood You supplied
You made me new
Clean and bright
We celebrate You now
As we remember Your sacrifice
Dying to sin
Then raising to life
Taking Your seat
as a King on the throne
Waiting patiently for Your people
Til the day You call us home

Jill

You are the sister
I chose for myself
You were there
when there was no one else
You built me up
You believed in me
You saw the potential
In who I could be
You always showed up for me
In so many ways
You've given me more love
Than I could ever repay
You are the person I need
when I feel about to fall
when something amazing or awful happens
you are always my first call
I have a family
and other friends, it's true
But there's a soul connection
that draws me closest to you
No matter the distance
or time between us
you will always have
my unconditional love
It may have taken us some time

to grow into ourselves
But I wouldn't have wanted to face that struggle
with anyone else
I love you, my sister
my very best friend
to the moon, to the stars
to whatever end.

Barbie

Thank you for being
exactly who you are
for being who I need
when I'm falling apart
For not judging me
even though I can be a little bit raw
for not nitpicking and focusing
on my every little flaw
Thank you for never hesitating
when I need you the most
when I call out for help
you are always the first to show
You are always calm and collected
when I'm a storm at sea
You could have any friend that you want
And I'm so grateful you want me
Our friendship isn't an everyday phone call
Or a drink at the bar
It's an I'll be there whenever you need me
No matter where or how far
You are the person I trust
to raise our little girl
should her Father and I
ever have to leave this world
You are the person I can worship with

The friend to pray beside me
To give me hard truths when I need them
To encourage my dreams
I'm so thankful to God
for putting us together
You are the truest of friends
You are stuck with me now and forever

Christina

I am so lucky
to have a sister like you
you weren't born of my Mother
But instead the sister I choose
You care about my family
You've never let me down
When I desperately need help
You are always around
You made me love to read again
You're always up for a good time
You're always there to extend your hand
when I am falling behind
I can always count on you
to give me sound advice
to show up if I call you crying
even if it's the middle of the night
I don't think you realize at all
The blessing really you truly are
You are as rare a person as they come
And more beautiful than the brightest star
Thank you for choosing me back dear sister
It's my honor to walk this life by your side
Blood might be thicker than water
But it's water that keeps us alive

Alex

You are the fire to my water
The mysterious darkness to my light
You are the warm blanket on a crisp cold
evening
The sharp blade I keep close to my side
You are the laughter I can't keep in
In the most inappropriate place
You are the truth that desperately needs to be
said
You are strength clothed in beauty and grace
You have walls built all around you
Impenetrable and damn near impossible to climb
But worth the effort for those brave enough to
dare
to see the most amazing person on the other side
You are funny, creative and thoughtful
You are hardworking, intelligent and kind
You're the friend anyone would be blessed to
have
I'm so thankful you chose to be mine.

Brian

How do I love you
let me count the ways
For one, you've given me the life of my dreams
Blessing me for all of my days
For two, you are the most loyal partner
For three, you so carefully hold my heart
For four, you give the best hugs on earth
For five, I can tell you hate whenever we part
For six, you make me laugh so hard
Especially when you don't try
For seven, you are always there to wipe my tears
For the million times a day that I cry
For eight, you love the Lord, our God
For nine, you always lend a helping hand
For ten, you always indulge my dreams
For eleven, you are such a great man
This rhyme could go on forever
I don't even think I could count high enough
To list all the ways you are incredible
Or to count all the ways you are loved

Take the leap

Don't be afraid
to try something new
you'll only regret
what you didn't do
It doesn't matter if you fail
You won by trying at all
Just run the race the best you can
don't focus on the fall
Give yourself the grace
to make a few mistakes
don't give up if you don't succeed at first
try again as often as it takes
Realize that almost anything worth it
will rarely come easily
That things that are truly valuable
Are hardly, if ever, free
The work is part of the path we take
the change in you happens on the road
The destination is just the payoff
But the journey is where you grow
Be proud of even the smallest wins
Please don't ever lose heart
Even if you feel like have so far to go
You at least had the courage to start
Some people never leave their comfort

never take a chance on themselves
don't worry about what anyone has to say about
you
You have only to prove who you are to yourself

Who I am

I love music, steak and sunsets
I love God, my family and friends
I love deep conversations about nothing at all
I love a cold room with a warm blanket and bed
I love singing, dancing and reading
I love writing and drawing, as well
I love getting together with girlfriends
Sharing secrets we'll never tell
I love cuddling with my husband
I love putting my daughter to bed
I love our bedtime routine
praying together, as she rests her head
I love movies, chocolate and long hugs
I love babies and puppies too
I love taking pictures of flowers
but mostly, I love all of you